"The world is a book, and those who do not travel
read only a page." -Saint Augustine

BUDAPEST

72 Hours in Budapest

A smart swift guide to delicious food, great rooms and what to do in Budapest, Hungary.

TRIP PLANNER GUIDES

TABLE OF CONTENTS

	Before You Get Started…	7
1	Welcome to Budapest	9
2	Budapest Neighborhoods & How Not to Get Lost	23
3	Daily Itinerary Planner	34
4	Day One Tour: An Unforgettable Introduction To Budapest	35
5	Day Two Tour: The New & Old Budapest	42
6	Best Budapest Experiences for Day Three	50
7	Unique Budapest Experiences	58
8	Budapest By Night	62
9	Best Day Trips from Budapest	68
10	A Day Out Shopping in Budapest	72
11	Budapest Local Cuisine	75
12	Dining Out in Budapest	79

13 Accommodation Guide   87

14 Budapest Travel Essentials   93

15 Hungarian Language Essentials   97

    Conclusion   103

BEFORE YOU GET STARTED

We've put together a quick set of tips for maximizing the information provided in this guide.

Insider tips: Found in italics throughout the guide, these are golden nuggets of information picked up during our travels. Use these handy tips to save money, skip the queues and uncover hidden gems.

Maps: This guide connects you to the most up-to-date city and transport maps. Step-by-step instructions are included on how to access. We highly recommend reviewing these maps PRIOR to departing on your trip.

Itineraries: While we have enclosed memorable itineraries for your use, we understand that sometimes you just want to venture out on your own. That is why all major attractions, hotels, restaurants and entertainment venues are tagged with the neighborhood that houses them. In doing so, you'll know what's nearby when planning your adventures.

Budget: Prices at time of publication are provided for all major attractions and a pricing scale is provided for all hotels, restaurants and entertainment.

Websites: To ensure you have the most up-to-date information prior to departure we have included links to venue websites for your convenience. Simply enter the url into your favorite browser to load the webpage.

1 WELCOME TO BUDAPEST

Budapest, the capital of Hungary, is a blissful hub drenched in natural beauty, an enticing culture, and interesting history. Of all the major European capitals this is the one which tends to surprise foreign visitors the most. They've heard of it (maybe) and they may even have seen photos of its stunning cityscape, yet many are still left pleasurably astounded by how wonderful this city can be.

Famous for its youthful vibe and it stability to fuse old with new, this Hungarian gem boasts a plethora of varied attractions, including a vibrant nightlife that will keep you grooving until the wee hours of the morning. Yet, for its buzz and energy, the city remains a laid-back sanctuary; an unpretentious riverside village, at heart. For lovers of history, culture, great food, amazing architecture, good shopping and nature, this all-encompassing destination is ideal. Underrated and overlooked by many, Budapest is a hidden European treasure.

Aside from taking relaxing strolls along the shores

of the Danube River or admiring the opulent imperial palaces of yesteryear, Budapest offers infinite opportunities to delve into its phenomenal traditional cuisine, whose many specialties date back to the Austro-Hungarian period. Infused with flavours of its neighbouring countries, local Hungarian cuisine can be both familiar and utterly unique.

The abundance of hot thermal natural baths, for which the city is internationally renowned, have given rise to the nickname "The City of Spas", adding yet another enticing angle to what will surely be an unforgettable trip.

The city of Budapest is indeed a beautiful, vibrant and colourful destination set to bombard your senses in a myriad of ways. After all, it was listed as a UNESCO World Heritage Site in 1987, for the architectural and cultural significance of its historic centre.

So, if you are looking for an eclectic destination that can rival Paris and other top destinations worldwide, look no further than Budapest.

A Brief Look Back in Time

Budapest boasts an eclectic history and spent much of its time either being invaded or liberated. Its beginnings were humble and the modern-day city, which was once a trio of small enclaves called Obuda, Pest and Buda, was not formed until 1873.

Archaeological finds have dated human existence here to the Stone Age, with very definite proof of settlement, on both sides of the Danube, as far back as 2,000 BC. A flourishing Roman fort was built in Obuda in 200BC and, although the Romans only held ground here for two centuries, their influence is still visible nowadays.

Once the Roman Empire collapsed in the 4th century, it allowed the Huns and other tribes to settle in the territory. In the 9th century, the Magyars, the ancestors of today's Hungarians, settled in the Carpathian Basin along the Danube River. Spearheaded by St. Stephen (Hungary's first king), the Magyars established a strong state in this region which lasted well into the Middle Ages. With the arrival of the brutal Mongols, the city – and the entire country in fact – suffered its first devastating invasion. The Mongols decimated the Magyar population and burnt their crops, causing catastrophic famine countrywide. Whether by sword or hunger, the Mongols are credited with killing off half of Hungary's entire population, during their terrifying conquest of Eastern Europe.

Once the Mongols finally retreated back to the Far East, King Bela IV restored the country in the 13th century and built a strong fortress on the hills of Buda, bolstering defence against future raids. It wasn't until the 15th century that Buda truly flourished, and these years are considered the Golden Era of the city, as it became the epicentre of arts, culture and politics in contemporary Europe. Pest, on the other hand, was viewed as the commercial centre of the country.

The enclaves were once again thrown into turmoil, when the Turks arrived in 1526. They settled in Budapest for over a century and introduced a handful of exotic traditions to the Hungarians. They took to converting churches into mosques, built Ottoman-era bath houses and left a most defining 'Eastern touch' to the city. Nowadays, Budapest is home to the most beautiful Turkish baths outside of Turkey.

Trail-blazed by the Roman Emperor, a Christian army liberated Pest and Buda in 1686. Unfortunately, both towns were destroyed in this siege. Even Castle Hill's glittering Royal Palace was left in ruins following the so-called rescue. To make matters worse, the siege didn't bring freedom to the country, as it was anointed as one of the provinces of the Habsburg Empire. Independence did not arrive until 1867. Just six years later, Budapest was finally founded and declared the capital of Hungary, flourishing once again...right up until WWI.

As the new empire was propelled into the First World War, and once again involved in the second, Budapest seemed to somehow survive, showing its infinite resilience amidst the devastating chaos and destruction which ensured.

Over the last two decades, it has once again risen and is now considered one of Europe's most enticing and captivating holiday destinations.

Not hard to see why that would be.

Climate & Best Time to Visit

Sheltered by the Alps and isolated by the
Carpathian Basin, Budapest has a temperate climate
that favours sightseeing at any time of year.
Although the climate does tend to be a lot more
stable year-round than many other European
capitals, tourist crowds ebb with the holiday flow.
As a result, some seasons are indeed better than
others, if you wish to enjoy the city in relative calm.
For this reason, Spring and Autumn are, by far, the
most enjoyable periods in which to visit Budapest.

Here is an overview of the seasons and the best time
to visit:

Winter: December-February

Breezy, overcast and dreary, Budapest in winter is
very much a love-it or hate-it affair. Yes, it's oh-so
romantic to visit here in winter, but days are
painfully short and it's never a lot of fun to suffer
face-freeze while out and about walking the streets,
so visiting at this time, although it's the cheapest by
far, is very much a subjective decision. Budapest's
winters may not be as brutal as in other European
countries, but considering you'll want to spend
much time outdoors it probably isn't the ideal time
to visit. January is by far the coldest month, with

temps hovering around -1 ℃ (30 ℉), whilst December usually sees temperatures just a couple of degrees higher.

Spring: March to May

Everything about Spring is delightful in Budapest. Flowers are blooming, crowds are minimal and prices for both flights and accommodation much lower. Average temperatures hover around 23 ℃ (74 ℉). March is renowned for being unpredictable yet this should never be a deterrent, as downturns are usually fleeting.

Summer: June-August

Summers in Budapest are a lot more comfortable than other European cities, with temps rarely going above 30 ℃ (86 ℉). This is both the busiest *and* most expensive time of year to visit.

Insider's Tip: Budapest may be well off the tourist radar for North Americans, yet it always has been (and continues to be) a much coveted holiday destination for Europeans. Summer school holidays last three months in the continent (June-August) and, if you can help it all, avoiding this period is a really great idea.

Autumn: September to November

Superb is about the easiest way to describe
Budapest at this time. Crowds are dwindling,
gorgeous fall foliage in abundance and prices are,
once again, heading south fast. Average temps in
this period are a delightful 24 ºC (75 ºF).

Language

Packing an English-to-Hungarian dictionary is a
great idea, as it'll give you a chance to delve a little
deeper into the culinary delights offered. However,
locals are renowned for their friendliness and
hospitality, as well as for their English-speaking
skills, so ask for assistance should you need to.
Many will be very happy to help.

Getting In

Budapest can be reached in several ways, by plane,
train, bus or boat, with the latter being immensely
enjoyable, if not a tad expensive.

By Plane

The fastest and most convenient way to travel to
this capital is to take a plane ride bound for
Budapest Franz Liszt International Airport (BUD),
the largest airport in the country. As an international
airport, it connects Budapest to several international
cities in Middle East, Africa, America, and Europe,

and is serviced by many international airlines, including Air France, Japan Airlines and American Airlines. The international airport is about 15 km (9 miles) from the city centre.

http://www.bud.hu/

Insider's Tip: do note that there are no direct flights to Budapest from the USA, so you will have to plan a stopover in another European capital first. London and Amsterdam are the most popular choices. Want to save some precious holiday funds? Low-cost airlines like Easy jet and Ryan Air offer great deals from Berlin, London and Paris.

By Train

If you're planning a whirlwind European tour, check out RailEurope and the MAV (Hungarian National Railways) for great deals on both domestic and foreign train travel. Budapest boasts three major train stations - namely Keleti, Nyugati and Deli – with the former being the most popular.

RailEurope: http://tinyurl.com/raileuropebudapest

MAV: http://www.mavcsoport.hu/en

Insider's Tip: Train stations are renowned for being a little on the dodgy side, and Budapest's Keleti is no exception. If arriving here by train, be alert and keep a vigilant eye on all your belongings. Avoid arriving after sunset. Beware the 'helpful train staff scam', whereby petty criminals, looking very officious and wearing neon-vests, approach tourists offering help, and get nasty when you refuse to pay for their services at the end. Be aware of this issue and refuse to engage with anyone at the station, no matter how friendly and well-dressed they may appear.

By Coach

Operating under the management of Volan Association, Hungary has a national bus network that connects Budapest to all major cities in Hungary. Furthermore, there are a few bus companies that have routes to international destinations. Eurolines has daily trips from and to Slovakia and Austria. Orangeways, meanwhile, connects the city to Slovakia, Poland, Netherlands, Germany, Croatia, Czech Republic and Austria.

Volan: http://www.volan.eu/

Eurolines: http://www.eurolines.hu/en

Orangeways: http://www.orangeways.com/en

By Boat

You can reach Budapest by taking a hydrofoil service from Bratislava, Nuremberg or Vienna along a scenic route of the Danube River. This would have to be, between the months of April and November, the most enjoyable, relaxing and utterly stunning way to reach the Hungarian capital. Check out RiverCruiseAdvisor for trips from Germany, and Budapest.com for trips from Bratislava and Vienna.

River Cruise Advisor:
http://tinyurl.com/rivercruiseadvisor

Budapest.com River Travel Page:
http://tinyurl.com/budapestbyriver

Insider's Tip: Aside the fact that you'll end in Budapest, a Danube River cruise is a bucket-list worthy activity like no other. You'll pass dozens of locks, experience a min-boggling rise and fall in altitude and be privy to some of Eastern Europe's most spellbinding and historic cities. If you have time – and a bit of extra holiday cash – do consider reaching Budapest by river boat. It's pure magic.

Getting around

Are you a nomadic soul who loves to travel on foot? Then you've come to the right city!

Walking around Budapest's historic centres is by far the best and most effective way to get an insider's perspective of this fascinating place. Most of the city's top sites and attractions are within walking distance to each other, helping you reduce your transportation costs. As you make your way around the city on foot, just be sure to bring a paper map of the destination or a phone with a GPS.

Insider's Tip: want an amazing insider's intro into Budapest? Then book your spot on the <u>Free Budapest's Walking Tours</u>, the city's foremost tourist activity. Led by knowledgeable and enthusiastic guides, these tours are fun, informative and free? What more could one ask for?!

Free Walking Tours: http://www.triptobudapest.hu/

Not overly fond of walking? Thankfully, <u>BKV</u>, the city's public transportation system, offers cheap metro, tram, trolleybus, boat and bus services all over the city. Before you hop on a public transportation service, though, make sure to have your tickets validated, as inspectors impose hefty fines for invalidated tickets. Also, purchase your tickets ahead of time at a newsstand or metro station, as they might not be available on-board. Check out the website for info on timetables, as well as funicular info to reach Buda Castle.

BKV: http://www.bkv.hu/en/

Insider's Tip: European residents aged over 65 get to travel on all public transport free of charge, as long as they show ID verifying age and address.

<u>Prices</u>

Single fare tickets: 530 HUF

3-stop passes (without leaving the station): 300 HUF

24-hour passes (unlimited rides): 1,650 HUF

24-hour group passes (up to 5 people): 3,300 HUF (Ideal for families!)

72-hour passes: 4,150 HUF

72-hour group passes: 4,950 HUF

One-week pass: 4,950 HUF

Funicular to Castle Hill: 1,100 HUF

Chairlift: 850 HUF

Boat tickets (one-way): 750 HUF

NB. Prices are subject to change seasonally and yearly, so do check the website for the most updated prices and times before arriving in Budapest.

Do you want to drive around and explore the city at your own will? Renting a car may seem a viable option to get around the city but it's not as practical, and can be a bit inconvenient with the city's heavy traffic, especially in the late afternoons and mornings. Also, you need to have a solid know-how about their driving rules and etiquette.

Taxis are a dime a dozen in the city of Budapest. As a tourist, these cabs certainly can come in handy during your trip. However be sure to hire only a legitimate and regulated taxi, as there are many unauthorized taxi drivers who overcharge naïve travellers. The registered and genuine cabs are those with yellow taxi signs and license plates, as well as ID badges on their dashboards.

With Budapest's burgeoning network of cycling paths, it is no wonder more and more of the city's dwellers are using bicycles as their primary means of transportation. The city's main roads are a bit unnerving and busy for inexperienced cyclists, but there are a few areas where biking may be pleasurable, such as Margaret Island and City Park.

Hop-on/Hop-off Tours

There are two companies in Budapest which run hop-on/hop-off tours, both of which are quite well rated.

Big Bus & Giraffe run equally good torus, leading you along established tourist routes, to and past all major attractions. Giraffe may be the most popular one out of the two (marginally) which actually means their buses tend to get fuller, faster. Both offer free Danube River cruises and night-time tours, and both charge 22 Euros (6,825 HUF) for 48 hour tickets.

Big Bus:
http://eng.bigbustours.com/budapest/home.html

Giraffe: http://www.citytour.hu/en

Insider's Tip: Frugal travellers can save quite a bit of money by simply purchasing a multi-day public transport ticket and downloading a walking tour app. At the end of the day, you'll get the exact same thing for a lot less cash. Besides, buses, trams, metro and boats run much more frequently than either above-mentioned buses thus leaving you with less waiting-around time.

2 BUDAPEST NEIGHBORHOODS & HOW NOT TO GET LOST

Budapest is made up of 23 districts, with Buda and Pest, for obvious reasons, being the most well-known. Each borough bears a number indicated by Roman Numerals (i.e.: I, X, V, XXII), with lower numbers being around downtown, and higher ones being suburban outskirts.

Insider's Tip: If trying to locate a place/restaurant/hotel by a given address, note that the middle two numbers of the postcode denote the zone. Eg Zipcode 1129 means the establishment is in the 12th district.

The central areas for tourist activities are V, VI and VII and these are arguably the best areas in which to stay. Gentrified, safe, enticing and entertaining, you will end up spending much of your time here, especially if just visiting for a couple of days.

These are the most popular areas of Budapest:

District I: Buda

This is the hilly district found on the West side of the **Danube River** which divides the Buda & Pest neighbourhoods. Though more laid back than Pest, it is absolutely stunning. The **Castle District** (aka District I) is located atop Buda's Castle Hill, so expect healthy crowds throughout day.

District II: Vizivaros

Another neighbourhood within the Buda side is called **Vizivaros (Water Town)**, so named because of its location between the castle district and the river. Though mostly residential, you can consider hotels in this location as it is close to the castle district & has great transportation links throughout Budapest.

Nature enthusiasts should consider stopping by **Buda Hills** – a beautiful area that is famous for its caves and enormous summer homes and residential houses, it feels detached from city life -as if you are in the countryside, yet Buda Hills is also conveniently close to the city centre.

District V- Pest

Found on the East side of the Danube, Pest is home to the city center and famous tourist sites like **City Park & Szechenyi Baths**, among others. This is where two of the city's three main railway stations are found. The new main road, **Új Fő Utca**, is partly pedestrian-only and one of the latest renovations projects undertaken by the city' council. The **Great Market Hall** and famous **Vaci Streets** are also found here.

The historic inner core of Pest is called **Belvaros (The Inner City)** and this is where most tourists flock to, and a spot renowned for its pedestrian shopping street, and for the boulevards that connect it to various other suburbs throughout the city. If the bustling city centre gets too busy for you, consider heading to **Lipotvaros (Leopold Town)**, the central business district and political centre of Hungary. Originally established in the early 19th century, the town is dotted with multiple monuments, and home to grand historic buildings, the most beautiful of which is the **Parliament Building**.

District VI - Terézváros

Considered Budapest's high-end entertainment quarter, Terézváros is home of the internationally renowned Budapest Opera House, Music Academy and Operetta Theatre. Some of the most stunning mansions in the city are found here, wide along tree-lined avenues and accosting classy boutiques and super trendy cafés.

District VII - Erzsébetváros

The city's former Jewish Quarter is a buzzy place to visit and home to various synagogues, including the lovely Great Synagogue, and where you'll also find the **New York Palace on Grand Boulevard**. **Kazinzky Street** is the reputed nightlife hub of Budapest but this entire hood is brimming with great bars, cafes, pubs and clubs, so stay here if you prefer a lively and sociable base.

District VIII – Józsefváros

This is one of Budapest's most inhabited and perhaps poorest quarters. Although it tends to keep off most tourist's radar, it is an infinitely interesting suburb to explore at great length because it's the one which grants a more realistic and honest look into Hungarian way of life, away from the glitz of the capital and its renowned attractions. This district is home to the **main train station (Keleti)**, as well as a smattering of museums and lovely public gardens. A fantastic **Chinese market** gifts this hood a bit of an exotic feel. Do beware that this suburb boasts an unfortunately high rate of crime so be alert and don't walk alone at night and take cabs to get around after sunset. Do this, and Józsefváros can be an incredibly rewarding place to stay, and just as safe as the centre.

Insider's Tip: If you have particular interests, then join one of the great walking/cycling/Segway tours offered by Absolute Walking Tours – This is a paid walking tour but comes highly recommended nonetheless. They offer various tours which take in the city from different angles and concentrating on varying interests, whether that be history, culture or architecture. PS. If your travels take you to Prague, Krakow or Vienna you can also join their walking tours in either of these cities.

Absolute Walking Tours:
http://www.absolutetours.com/index-budapest.php

How to get your bearings and avoid getting lost

Budapest is a sprawling city; no doubt about that. Couple this with a local language that can be challenging to master and suddenly, you may it difficult to make your way around. If you think it can't get any worse, since the early 2010s, several historic places and as well as train stations and airports have been renamed, making it even more confusing for a typical visitor to figure their way around.

But we have a plan! Follow our tips on how best to avoid getting hopelessly lost in Budapest and, if everything fails, do keep in mind that being lost in a beautiful city like Budapest *still* beats sitting at your office desk. Win-win.

Orientation Tips:

1) If you are on a boat cruise along the Danube River or walking alongside it and forget which area of Budapest you are in, remember this: **Buda is**

hillier and is on the West of the river, while **Pest is the more commercialized** area that is located on the East. The north of Buda is called Obuda. If you managed to wander close to Obuda then you are technically in the outskirts of Budapest.

2) Aside from walking, the metro can be your best bet of getting to and from one tourist attraction to another, especially as it's convenient and inexpensive. There may be multiple exits per station, so make sure you **take note of the street name of the attraction you want to see and then follow the signs that will lead you to the correct exit**. If all else fails, pick a random exit then grab your map and try to get your bearings upon reading the street signs.

3) The tram is also an excellent way to pinpoint your location. **Tram #2 traverses the Pest side** of the Danube Embankment, where the beginning of the line is the Great Boulevard (near Margaret Bridge). This tram will pass through various other sites like the Parliament, Chain Bridge, and Great Market Hall. **Tram #19 and 41 on the other hand traverses the Buda side** of the Danube Embankment, going to Castle Hill then under Elisabeth Bridge. Depending where you are, you can hop on either of those trams mentioned that go to common tourist areas to get your bearings or find your way to your hotel.

4) Buses and trolleys also ply the streets, but may be a little more confusing to navigate unless you note the stop specifically. Take note of the following words when on public transportation: **A (direction) fele** – the direction where your bus/tram/metro is going. **Megallo** – stop/station. **Vegallomas** – end of the line (and you need to depart)

The city is home to quite a few tourist information centres, called **Budapestinfo Points**:

Tourist Information (TI) Sütő utca – the main tourist information centre, on Deák Square.
1052 Budapest, Sütő utca 2
Phone: (+36-1)438-8080
Mon-Sun: 8 am- 8 pm

TI Teréz körút
1061 Budapest, Teréz körút 2-4
Open: Mon-Fri: 10 am-6 pm

Tourinform Buda Castle – TourInform is the Hungarian National Tourist Office. This TI is across Matthias Church.
1014 Budapest, Szentháromság tér
Open: Mon. - Sun.: 9 am-6 pm

TourInform Műjég
1146 Budapest Olof Palme sétány 2.
Open: 9 am - 7 pm

Airport Locations:

Terminal 1
Open: Mon.-Sun.: 9 am-10 pm
Terminal 2A
Open: Mon.-Sun.: 8 am-11 pm

Terminal 2B
Open: Mon.-Sun.: 10 am-12 pm

Alternatively, you can call or email the TourInform hotlines if you are in need of help:

Tourinform hotline (24 hours):
Phone :(+36-30)30-30-600 from abroad, (06-80) 630-800 from Hungary
E-mail: hungary@tourinform.hu

Useful Maps & Websites

Where would we be without maps? Since the beginning of time, man has been gallivanting the globe with the use of maps and nowadays, despite the advent of GPS technology on our mobile phones, maps still play an integral part of travelling. It's always a great idea to bring along a few (old fashioned!) paper maps, as phone batteries can die unexpectedly.

Here are some important notes to remember:

-It's imperative that the maps you bring are up to date, as names of places and streets can change quite often in Budapest.

-Download and print maps from the web before you even arrive, and get acquainted with the city's layout and transport system before you decide where you'll stay.

Our list of the most useful online maps of Budapest:

General City Map

The Michelin Guide is a reat general map of the city, where you can zoom in to a particular area and print each section separately. If connected to the net abroad, use the interactive display to find restaurants, tourist attractions and hotels.

http://www.viamichelin.com/web/Maps/Map-Budapest

Public Transport Map

You'll find this interactive map on the BKK website super easy to use and print, by simply clicking on your desired city suburb. Check below for a comprehensive map of the Metro lines, as well as a broader map which incorporates the various public transport modes. The public transport boat routes are also detailed below.

BKK: http://www.bkk.hu/en/maps/

Metro: http://tinyurl.com/budapestmetro

Public Transport:
http://tinyurl.com/budapestpublictransport

Boat Routes: http://tinyurl.com/budapestboats

GPS MY City App

Use this fantastic app to download a Budapest map to your Smartphone, and use it offline.

My City App: http://tinyurl.com/mycitybudapest

Here are some websites you'll find useful when planning your trip, or once you are in Budapest already:

-Up-to-date weather reports:
http://budapest.travel/weather/

-Where/how to buy concert and opera tickets:
http://tinyurl.com/budapestconcert

-Concise online survival dictionary:
http://budapest.travel/info/survivaldic/

-Official Tourism Website:
http://en.budapestinfo.hu/

-Up-to-date currency converter:
http://tinyurl.com/budapestcurrency

3 DAILY ITINERARY PLANNER

Budapest on a long week-end

Is it possible to experience Budapest in three days?
The short answer is "Yes, of course, if that's all the
time you have" yet like many other cities of note,
with such an array of attractions and activities
staying for at least a week would be ideal.
But...hey...we can't have it all, right?

Looking for ideas on how you may best fill in your
days, and absorb as much of the city's essence as
you can?

We've got you covered! The following are full-day
itineraries to give you an idea of just how much (or
how little) you can expect to achieve in just a single
day. Feel free to mix and match attractions and,
using a list and a map, come up with your own
dream daily itinerary. You'll inevitably be unable to
tick off every box, and what better excuse to come
back and visit Budapest next year.

4 DAY ONE TOUR: AN UNFORGETTABLE INTRODUCTION TO BUDAPEST

For the first day of your trip to Budapest, you will be delving into the intriguing medieval history of the city with stops at monumental **Castle Hill (Varhegy),** home to Budapest's medieval heart and the most important UNESCO listed area in the entire city. Here, you can visit the **Royal Palace, Fisherman's Bastion** and **Matthias Church**.

Insider's Tip: Castle Hill can be 'done' leisurely in about 3-4 hours, although if you wish to visit any of the museums you'll come across you will need to add 2 more hours. Yes, it is ever so easy to simply spend an entire day here wandering about and even if you have more time, we suggest you do precisely this. Castle Hill is stunning, but it's also the most crowded and touristy spot in Budapest. Get it under your belt on your first day and you'll be free to explore the rest of the city. Do note that prices for food & drinks here are more expensive but grin and bear it for the day, or bring snacks to tide you over.

Here are the main attractions on Castle Hill, in **DISTRICT I**. You can reach the top of the hill on foot, by taking the Royal Steps from *Clark Ádám tér*, or take the funicular *Siklo'* from the other side of the Chain Bridge (*Széchenyi lánchíd*).

What to see: ROYAL PALACE

Overview of Activity: A wonderful place to walk around in, home of the Hungarian **National Gallery, Budapest History Museum, Lion Courtyard and National Library**.

Why you should go: Also known as **Buda Castle**, the former Royal Palace is a 13th century masterpiece of architecture and the city's riverside highlight. In the Middle Ages, this was the largest Gothic Palace in the country.

Directions: One of the city's most imposing sites, the Royal Palace is a little hard to miss. You'll find it along the Western shore of the Danube, next to the top station of the funicular cable-car.

Address: Szent-Gyorgy ter 6, Budapest 1014

Operating hours: The grounds are open to the public, but museums and galleries subject to their respective opening hours.

National Gallery: 10 am to 6 pm from Tuesday to Sunday.

History Museum: 10 am to 6 pm Tuesday to

Sunday (March to October), 10 am to 4 pm Tuesday to Sunday (November to February)

Website: http://budacastlebudapest.com/

Cost (in local currency): The Palace is free to explore at will, yet galleries and museums incur individual fees to enter.

History Museum: 2,000 HUF (*Are you an international student? Bring your student card ID and book your trip to coincide with the last weekend of the month. You'll get free entry into this museum on Saturday!*)

National Gallery: Permanent exhibits cost 1,000 HUF.

Temporary exhibits cost 2,000 HUF

Suggested arrival time & duration: 10 am – about an hour or two to enjoy the gardens and the spectacular views - if you plan on visiting the museum & gallery then add extra time.

Insider's Tip: While all three major attractions here, the palace grounds, museum and gallery, are well rated, the highlight of this section of Castle Hill would undoubtedly be the view. If you are short on time, then make this your 'vista enjoyment stop' but don't feel compelled to spend much time (or funds) to visiting every attraction here.

After spending a morning at the Royal Palace, your stomach may well be grumbling. Feast on a hearty and appetizing set lunch at one of Castle Hill's best bistros. Lunch for two will set you back about 5,000 HUF but consider the quality of the food, in the most touristy part of the city, the meals are actually worth every cent. Var Bistro boasts a great location, perfect vibe and friendly staff. Just super!

What: Var Bistro

Where: Disz Ter 8 | Disz Tér 8, Budapest 1014

Directions: As you exit the Palace, turn left and walk along *Szinhaz U.* for about 700 meters. You'll find Var Bistro on the northern end of *Disz Ter Park*.

Opening Hours: 8 am to 8 pm, 7 days a week

Website: http://tinyurl.com/varbistrobudapest

How Much: 5,000 HUF for a set lunch for two people, including drinks

For your next stop, you will be paying homage to one of the oldest buildings in the district, the **Matthias Church**.

What to see: MATTHIAS CHURCH – MATYAS TEMPLOM

Overview of Activity: Take in the visual spectacle of this most enchanting 14th century church, site of many royal events, including King's coronations and weddings.

Why you should go: Exquisite both in its exterior architecture and interior splendor, the church boasts the Hungarian Crown Jewels, gorgeous frescoes and stunning murals, alongside national priceless works of art.

Directions: The church is just a 4 minute walk north from Var Bistro in the main square, just one block south of the Hilton Budapest.

Address: Szentharomsag ter 2, Budapest 1014, Hungary

Operating hours: 9 am to 5 pm Monday to Friday. 9 am to 1 pm Saturday. 1 to 5 pm Sunday. Ticket booths shut 45 minutes before closing time

Phone #: +36 1 355 5657

Website:

www.matyas-templom.hu/main.php?Lang=EN

Cost (in local currency): 1,400 HUF for adults, free for children (6 yrs. and below), 1,000 HUF for students and seniors. Family ticket 3,300 HUF. Ticket includes entry into the **Museum of Ecclesiastical Art**.

Suggested arrival time & duration: 2 pm – one hour should suffice

Insider's Tip: It may seem strange to pay an entrance fee to visit a church, but once you step

inside and see the meticulous restoration work you'll be utterly impressed. Wavering on the ticket price? Don't! Budapest has few commanding religious attractions of note, so take full advantage. This church is worth its weight in plated gold.

Lauded as one of the most celebrated landmarks in Budapest, the **Fisherman's Bastion** is a splendid terrace which attracts hordes of tourists every day. While the landmark is only a hundred years old, most viewers think it's much older, due to its rustic design and style. Blending perfectly with the cobbled streets and buildings in Castle Hill, this 19th-century building has a touch of medieval to it, thanks to its neo-Gothic design.

What to see: FISHERMAN'S BASTION

Overview of Activity: Enjoy the superlative views and explore the enticing towers of the bastion.

Why you should go: Reminiscent of Disney World's fairytale castles, the bastion is an absolute sightseer's delight, with its classy turrets and pointed towers. Furthermore, it is a terrific vantage point from where to enjoy dramatic views of the Danube River and the entire city.

Directions: Directly in front of Matthias Church, in the main square of Castle Hill

Address: Tarnork Utca 28, Budapest, Hungary

Operating hours: This attraction is always open

Phone #: +36 1 458 3030

Website: http://www.fishermansbastion.com/

Cost (in local currency): The 7, 140-meter towers and most of its balconies are open to the public for free. The turrets and upper towers, however, have a small and affordable entrance fee of 700 HUF

Suggested arrival time & duration: 3pm – two hours (there are great souvenir shops here, as well as many amazing photo ops, especially of the city and Matthias Church behind it)

The best vantage points of the bastion are, perhaps unsurprisingly, taken up by overpriced cafés. Nevertheless, if you feel like splurging on a coffee without bothering about the price, this would be a great place to indulge.

After such a full day of sightseeing, it may be time to retreat back to your hotel, take a refreshing shower and rest, and head out again for a wonderful taste of Budapest by night. Don't forget to check out our chapter for the most interesting activities to indulge in after sunset.

On your way down to the city's centre, don't forget to take a relaxing stroll over **Chain Bridge**, one of the city's most recognizable landmarks and the most famous connection between Buda and Pest. This late 19th century suspension bridge measures over 1,000 meters and was, at the time of its construction, only the second permanent bridge built over the entire length of the Danube.

5 DAY TWO TOUR: THE NEW & OLD BUDAPEST

Most foreign tourists head to Budapest with a clearly defined list of must-see attractions, most of which are historical and ancient. Although paying homage to the city's history is certainly worthwhile, it also pays to acknowledge the very modern side of this fabulous city. Budapest is home to some of the most striking contemporary architecture in Europe, and this very mix of old and new is what makes the city so very unique.

Start your day's exploration at **Liberty Square (Szadadsag Ter)** which you'll find close to the Parliament Building. This gorgeous square and park, one of the city's foremost green areas, is flanked by impressive buildings, like the marble and glass Bank center, Stock Exchange Palace and National Bank of Hungary.

What to see: LIBERTY SQUARE - SZADADSAG TER

Overview of Activity: Public square and gardens, an ideal place for a morning stroll

Why you should go: This is one of Budapest center's most relaxing spots and a great place in which to people watch, aside admiring the surrounding architecture and Soviet-era monuments

District: V - Pest

Directions: You'll find this square on the eastern banks of the Danube, just three blocks back from the shore, half way between the Kossuth Lajos Ter and Arany Janos utca Metro Stations

Address: 1054 Szabadsag ter 7, Budapest, Hungary

Suggested arrival time & duration: 9 am – an hour or so

The most striking of all modernist buildings in Budapest, belongs to ING Insurance and you'll find their shiny, resplendent headquarters just 3.5kms east of Liberty Square, right across the road from **Vajdahunyad Castle**. Lovers of all architectural designs will be suitably impressed at this masterpiece of contemporary architecture.

What to see: ING BUILDING

Why you should go: To admire the distorted and eye-catching design of this award-winning building

District: VI - Pest

Directions: Either take a leisurely half-hour walk along Podmaniczky U. or take a cab.

Address: Budapest, Dózsa György út 84/b

Suggested arrival time & duration: 10.30 am – 20 minutes or so

Once you're ready, make your way back toward the waterfront and stop by the revered **Hungarian National Museum**. This museum is simply ideal for anyone who wants to learn more about the country's history, the displays are chronological, well made and exceptionally interesting. You can literally walk through the full history and making of this fascinating country. Permanent exhibits include the Coronation Mantle, ceramics, metalwork, weapons, textiles and furniture. Besides, the building itself boasts a striking neo-classic architectural design that will leave you in awe.

What to see: HUNGARIAN NATIONAL MUSEUM

Overview of activity: Admire the country's best and largest collections of art, history and archaeology

Why you should go: The oldest museum in Hungary, this historic place displays collections from areas which are nowadays, not within their borders.

District: VIII – Museum Quarter

Directions: To make your way back west, you can either take bus # 74 from *Dembinszky utca* all the way to the Hotel Astoria (from here, the museum is only one block south) or take a taxi for an easy 10 minute ride

Address: Muzeum korut 14-16, Budapest IX

Website: http://hnm.hu/en

Contact number: +36 1 338 2122

Opening hours: 10 am to 6 pm from Tuesday to Sunday

Cost (in local currency): 1,600 HUF, 500 HUF for seniors and students, free for children 6 years and under as well as anyone over 70 years of age.

Suggested arrival time & duration: 11.30 am – two hours

Time for lunch yet? Surely!

The Museum Quarter boasts quite a few excellent eateries and cafés, including **Caffe Torino**, a local and expat favourite joint boasting amazing Italian treats. You'll find this cozy café right next door to the museum and, with outdoor seating, a varied menu and truly wicked coffee; it's a great place to visit at any time of the day and is one of the city's most treasured hidden gems.

What: CAFFE TORINO

Where: Brody Sandor Street 2

District: VIII – Museum Quarter

Phone: +36 30 303 9466

Opening Hours: 8 am to 8.30 pm

Website: http://tinyurl.com/caffetorinobudapest

Specials: Panini, antipasti, pastries, wide selection of good coffee

Cost (in local currency): 4,000 HUF for lunch and coffee

Suggested arrival time & duration: 1.30 pm – one hour

Józsefváros is the exciting, soon to be gentrified District VIII of Budapest. Although wisdom would have kept you away just a few years ago, the tide (and reputation) of this interesting suburb is swiftly changing. Once the opulent pride and joy of the city was left in all but ruins for many decades, and although this corner of the city may seem decrepit at first sight, it hides some rather magnificent architectural gems if you look beyond the lack-lustre façade.

Enjoy strolling the streets, starting from **Mikszath Kálmán Square** and one of its many trendy cafés, and look for the most noted buildings in the area, like the **Hungarian Radio, Italian Cultural Centre and Hotel Palazzo Zichy**, one of the finest accommodation options in Budapest. More than anything, though, Józsefváros offers you the enviable chance to take a peek into the real, gritty side of authentic Budapest, something which is bound to disappear in the next few years. See it before it's gone forever.

What: JOZSEFVAROS

District: VIII

Why you should go: Lesser visited, more authentic and arguably more insightful than the more touristy districts of Budapest.

Directions: District VIII stretches for a couple of miles on the Pest side of the Danube, from Rakoczit ut in the north to Orczy Ut in the south, and as far east as Fiumei ut. From Caffe Torino and the National Museum, you can reach Mikszath Kálmán Square by walking for 500m south-east, just one block down Muzeum ut.

Suggested arrival time & duration: 3 pm – two hours

By the time your tour de force through the 8th district is over you may just want to leisurely make your way back to your hotel for a rest. Head back up to downtown along the Danube and end your day's exploration at the city's foremost attraction, the utterly stunning **Hungarian Parliament Building (Orszaghaz)**.

Built at the turn of the 20th century, this is one of

Europe's oldest government buildings and is, nowadays, arguably the most photographed building in Budapest. It helps, of course, that one can see it from just about anywhere along the riverfront, and the adjoining hills, as well as the fact that it boasts an immensely beautiful façade. The building took over two decades to complete and, in a twist of morose fate, the head architect, who had won an international bid for the honor of designing it, went blind just before his masterpiece was completed. Today, the Hungarian Parliament is the country's largest, and its capital's tallest, structure.

Insider's Tip: One could easily end every day in Budapest at this building, as the sunset views and sun glow are mesmerizing. Do note, however, that English-language tours of the interior are very worthwhile, so although admiring it from the outside is splendid, touring it extensively on the inside, with a knowledgeable guide, is highly interesting too. NB. Tours book out very, very fast so make sure you book your time slot at least 2 days in advance!

What to see: HUNGARIAN PARLIAMENT BUILDING

Overview of activity: Admire the glorious design of this building and take a guided tour inside if you have time. Note that the building cannot be toured without a guide.

Why you should go: This is arguably the most

beautiful – and definitely the most important – building in the country

District: V - Downtown

Directions: The Hungarian Parliament Building is right in the heart of Budapest's waterfront center. The Metro stops on its southern end (line M2, Kossuth Lajor Ter Stop), as does the Tram (line #2, Kossuth Lajor Ter Stop), while River Boat D13 will drop you off right out front.

Address: 1055 Budapest Kossuth Lajos Ter 1-3, Magyarorszag

Website: http://www.parlament.hu/en/web/house-of-the-national-assembly

Contact number: +36 1 441 4000

Opening hours: 8 am to 6 pm (Summer) – 8 am to 4 pm (Winter)

Cost (in local currency): EU citizens – 2,000 HUF (students – 1,000 HUF)

Non-EU citizens 5,200 HUF (students – 2,600 HUF)

Kids under 6 get in free

Suggested arrival time & duration: 6 pm for great sunset views – an hour is enough

8 am for guided tours – two hours at least

6 BEST BUDAPEST EXPERIENCES FOR DAY THREE

While you're planning your own daily itineraries, keep in mind that Budapest boasts enough attractions to fill in weeks' worth of touring. Do note that museums are free to enter on National Holidays, so take advantage of this if your vacation happens to run over a special celebration in Budapest.

These are the city's *other* main highlights, which you definitely should try to include in your itinerary. Here are the best experiences to be had in the city on your final day.

Danube River Cruise – The most incredible way to see the city is from the water. If you can manage nothing else, take in a sightseeing cruise along the Danube.

Insider's Tip: The sunset river cruises in Budapest are among the most popular activities in the city and, usually, are priced higher than daytime or after-dark cruises. Save your pennies and take a cruise after sunset instead, when you'll have the chance to see this city lit up like an enormous Christmas tree. The city has plenty of sunset viewing spots, yet seeing all the splendours by night is something special indeed. Mahart and Legenda both offer sightseeing cruises, whilst Eurama offer convenient hop-on/hop-off cruising options. Moreover, there is a passenger commuter ferry which plies the river route. Travel on this is included in your 24 or 72-hour pass and, although there's no commentary it really matters very little...when you end up getting a river cruise for free!

Mahart: http://www.mahartpassnave.hu/en

Legenda: http://legenda.hu/en

Eurama: http://tinyurl.com/euramabudapest

Shoes on the Danube – This riverside memorial was created to honour the Jews who lost their lives here during the Holocaust. Prisoners were forced to walk on the wharf and remove their shoes. They were then shot and thrown into the Danube. A very touching tribute.

Where: Pest side of the Danube Promenade, District V

St Stephen's Basilica – named in honour of Hungary's first King, this Roman Catholic Church was consecrated in 1905 and its striking neoclassical design makes this one of the world's most photographed buildings.

Where: Szent István tér 1, District V

http://www.bazilika.biz/

Hungarian State Opera House – Opened in 1884 to much acclaim, the national opera house is a Renaissance stunner of colossal proportions. If you can manage it, book a ticket to an opera here as the acoustics are said to be unrivalled.

Where: Andrássy út 22, District VI

http://www.opera.hu/programme

Gellert Hill – A 235mt high hill overlooking the city, this hill gifts arguably the very best views of the Danube and beyond.

Gellert Hill Cave – According to legend, this interesting network of caves was once the home of a hermit who healed the sick with the thermal water of a nearby lake. A chapel was constructed inside the cave, which still holds official religious ceremonies for Pauline Monks.

Margaret Island – A small, 2km long island found right in the middle of the Danube, Margaret Island is a lovely place to explore for the day. Historical ruins, fountains, gardens, bars and outdoor cafés amke this one of Budapest's most pleasurable nooks.

Miniversum – Showcases model displays of Hungary, Austria and Germany which have been reconstructed to $1/100^{th}$ of their original size, boasting interactive displays and lots of activities for curious children.

Where: Andrássy út 12, District VI

http://www.miniversum.hu/en/

Budapest Zoo & Botanical Gardens – initially opened in 1886 this is one of the world's oldest animal sanctuaries and nowadays home to over one thousand different species from every corner of the globe.

Where: Állatkerti krt. 6-12, District XIV

http://www.zoobudapest.com/en

Heroes' Square – The Square features the statues of the Seven Chieftains of the Magyars and several other national leaders. Open 24 hours.

Where: Hősök tere, District XIV

Great Synagogue – The beauty of the synagogue, one of the largest in the world, hides a heavy history, mainly from the World War II era where thousands took refuge to escape during the cold war winters. Times vary, however summer hours 10AM-5:30PM

Where: Dohány u. 2, District VII

http://www.greatsynagogue.hu/gallery_syn.html

Vajdahunyad Castle – Built in 1908, the castle inspired by Romania's Vajdahunyad Castle was meant to celebrate 1,000 years of Hungarian unification. Open 10AM – 5PM, closed Mondays.

Where: Vajdahunyad vár, District XIV

http://www.vajdahunyadcastle.com/

Andrassy Avenue – A great shopping and dining avenue filled with so much history, it was designated as a UNESCO World Heritage Site.

Where: Andrássy út 9, District VI

Gresham Palace – An Art Nouveau stunner, the

Gresham Palace was built as a residential building in 1906, but is now the Four Seasons Hotel. It was used in WWII as a barracks for the Soviet Army, and has recently been luxuriously renovated so that the beauty of the interior matches the grand exterior. Façade open 24/7.

Where: Széchenyi István tér 5-6, District V

http://www.fourseasons.com/budapest/

City Park – A charming public park near the center of Budapest, it's close to Heroes' Square, a zoo, Vajdahunyad Castle and several museums. Opening time to various sites within the park vary.

Where: Kós Károly stny, District XIV

Danube Promenade – One of the best walks in Budapest, this promenade stretches from the Elizabeth Bridge to the Chain Bridge right alongside the Danube. There are numerous cafes, restaurants and hotels along this walk, but also historical statues and a concert hall.

Where: Dunakorzó, Budapest Pest, City Center, District V

Hungarian National Gallery – This is the national art museum of Hungary, located inside Buda Castle.

It contains many important pieces of Hungarian art dating back to the 15th century. Open 10AM – 6PM, closed Mondays.

Where: Szent György tér 2, District I

http://www.mng.hu/en

TOP CHOICE <u>The House of Terror</u> *– Not the most jovial attraction in Budapest but an absolute must-visit for anyone interested in the tumultuous and painful history of this country, which endured decades of brutal fascist dictatorship.*

Where: Andrássy út 60, District VI

http://www.terrorhaza.hu/

Lukacs Baths – Budapest is a city known for medicinal thermal baths, and Lukacs is one of the most historic, as it has been in operation for almost a thousand years. Open 6AM – 9PM

Where: Frankel Leó út 29, District II

http://www.bathsbudapest.com/lukacs-bath

Szechenyi Baths – Europe's largest medicinal thermal bath is housed in a beautiful century-old palace.

Where: Állatkerti krt. 9-11, District XIV

http://www.szechenyibath.hu/

Insider's Tip: there's a whole cultural rigmarole involved in a 'day at the spa in Budapest', so it helps to be prepared. Although you may want to experience the lesser-touristy baths, for a more authentic soak, do note that info in English here will be sadly lacking. Note that mixed sex spas demand you wear a swimsuit, whilst single-sex spas demand you go in your birthday suit instead. You'll be provided with a thin robe to walk about in. Make sure you know what your selected spa requires, by asking your hotel concierge to call ahead and gather details for you. It may save you some embarrassment! Moreover, do note that most baths will offer a refund on entry fee is you leave within 2 hours but, unless you ask specifically (which you should!) they may not openly advertise this.

7 UNIQUE BUDAPEST EXPERIENCES

Budapest is a lot more than the sum of all its priceless monuments, buildings and castles. The local culture is an intoxicating mix of east and west, new and old, and taking some time to delve into it a little deeper is one of the most rewarding things you could do. So once you've seen this, visited that and photographed the other, include some of these very authentic and unique Budapest experiences in your itinerary.

Revel in a folkloric dance performance

The Danube Palace Theatre holds regular performances by one of Budapest's best folkloric performance groups. Enjoy a sensational and mesmerizing evening of music and dance, which is set to be a highlight on any visit to the Hungarian capital.

What: 1.5 hr performance by The Hungarian State Folk Ensemble

Website: http://www.heritagehouse.hu/mane/#_=_

How: Book online in advance or ask your hotel to organize tickets and have them ready at your hotel upon arrival.

Where: Danube Palace Theatre

http://www.ticket.info.hu/en/program/theatres-venues/duna-palota

Budapest, Zrínyi u. 5, 1051

District V

+36 1 317 2754

8 am to 10 pm

Directions: The Danube Palace Theatre is located just one block back from the waterfront, directly opposite Castle Hill and just behind the Four Seasons Hotel, in District V. Buses #15 and 115 stop directly in front of the theatre.

How Much: Prices range from 3,000 HUF to 6,600 HUF depending on performance

Have an authentic Hungarian, Turkish bath

This may seem like an oxymoron, but the Turkish influence in the country has remained ever since the Ottomans conquered the country many moons ago. Renowned as Europe's spa capital, Budapest is home to many thermal baths reputed to have wonderful therapeutic effects.

What: A wide selection of therapeutic treatments at Rudas Baths

Website: http://en.rudasfurdo.hu/#_=_

How: Purchase your ticket online or visit the bath

Where: Dobrentei ter 9, Budapest 1016

District: I

When: Every day from 6 am to 10 pm

Women only on Tuesday, men only on all other weekdays

Weekends are group sessions

Directions: The spa is located right at the base of the Elizabeth Bridge, on the Buda side

How Much: From 2,400 HUF to 4,990 HUF depending on day/time of visit and included treatment

Enjoy a Hungarian Cooking Class

There's really no better way to get to know a new culture than through your taste buds, are we right? Spare some time during your visit to Budapest and indulge in a gastronomic experience like no other. Learn to cook authentic Hungarians meals in the comfort of a local's home, experience the genuine hospitality, and incredible cooking skills, of this wonderful people.

What: Home cooking class and market tour with Culinary Hungary Home Cooking Class

Website: http://budapestcookingclass.com/#_=_

Phone: +36 20 779-3375

When: 9 am to 3 pm, any day you'd like

How: Contact Agnes and Andrew to discuss your options, as classes can be suited to your personal needs

Where: Forint Street, Budapest 1024

District II

Directions: Forint Street is on the Buda side of the Danube, just one block west of the Millenaris Park. Bus # 149 will take you just one block south of Forint U.

How Much: A private class consisting of a market tour and hands on cooking class costs 35,000 HUF per person – and worth every Forint! Payment is made at the end of the class, in cash

8 BUDAPEST BY NIGHT

When nightfall rolls in, the city of Budapest shifts gears, transforming into a heaven for socialites and night owls. From plush dance clubs to open-air music lounges and ethereal jazz bars, Budapest bombards party goers with a nightlife scene to suit everyone's taste.

District VII is particularly revered for boasting fantastic clubs, and unique 'ruin pubs', which have been set up in the crumbling ruins of buildings scattered throughout this historic Jewish Quarter. Drawing a trendy and young crowd, this district has a buzzing bohemian scene, and a handful of modish spots can also be found in Kiraly, Wesselenyi and Dob utcas.

On the Buda part, the River Danube's bank offers fun boat clubs and bars with lively and young crowds. Do you love to gamble? The city has a surfeit of casinos housed in luxury hotels between the Elizabeth Bridge and Chain Bridge, and along Dunakorzo.

Budget: With Budapest being the affordable city it

is, enjoying a night out here is never going to hurt the pocket (too much), when compared to other major European cities. Expect drinks to cost about 1,400 HUF, and that's in the tourist center of Downtown. Most clubs and bars also are not in the habit of charging an entry fee – which is great – but may require you purchase a separate ticket if they have a particularly popular band playing. Nevertheless, this usually does not amount to more than the price of a drink. So head off and enjoy in style, as this is one of the continent's most affordable, and rewarding, capital cities.

The ruin-pub which started the trend

What: Szimpla Kert

Where: Kazinczy utca 14, Budapest 1075, Hungary

District VI

Website: http://www.szimpla.hu/

Phone: +36 1 352 4198

When: 12 pm to 4 am every day

Why: The undisputed star of the city's glamorous nightlife scene and admired for its eccentric style, this venue is a revolutionary ruin-pub embellished with diverse remnants of Hungary's communist-era. Besides its terrific atmosphere and quirky decorations, the club has fantastic live music and cheap drinks as well.

Insider's Tip: Szimpla Kert may be all glitzy now it's hit superstardom, but note that ruin-pubs are actually renowned for being not unlike undercover pubs, although there's nothing at all illegal about them, it is just the pure essence of what they are. From the outside they look like perfectly innocuous homes, with no signs, bright lights, blaring music or crowds hanging about. Yet step inside and out to the back courtyard however, and a whole new social party scene opens up to you. Want to go on a ruin-pub crawl when in Budapest? Then check out this fantastic website: http://ruinpubs.com/ which constantly updates its list of the coolest, newest and best ruin-pubs in town.

Manufactured surrealism with mind-blowing music

What: Instant

Where: Nagymezo u. 38, Budapest 1065, Hungary

District VI

Website: http://instant.co.hu/

Phone: +36 1 311 0704

When: 4 pm to 6 am

Why: A euphoric labyrinth with a dreamlike setting, Instant has over three bustling dance floors, six bars and 2 gorgeous outdoor gardens. Instant boasts free entrance and twisting pathways with strange yet beautiful decorations. Jazz, Indie and rock are usually on the musical menu here.

A spoonful of hard rock music

What: Club 202

Where: Fehervari ut 202, 1116 Hungary

District I

Website: http://www.club202.hu/

 Phone: +36 1 208 5569

When: Check out their FB Page for upcoming events.

Why: This is Budapest's best live rock music hall, which regularly hosts live concerts and gigs from the country's best hard rock bands.

A trendy rooftop club with a zesty dance club

What: Corvinteto

Where: Blaha Lujza ter 1-2, Budapest, Hungary

District VIII

Website: http://corvinteto.hu/

Phone: +36 20 378 2988

When: 6 pm to 5 am Monday to Sunday

Why: One of the hottest rooftop bars in the city, which even received a mention in the New York Times, Corvinteto has reached the national limelight for its dynamic underground dance club, superb city skyline views, and affordable prices.

Hungarian jazz music at its best…and then some!

What: Budapest Jazz Club

Where: Hollan Erno utca 7, Budapest 1136, Hungary

District I

Website: http://www.bjc.hu/

Phone: +36 70 413 9837

When: 6 pm to 4 am from Monday to Saturday. Closed on Sundays

Why: A true jazz-lover's delight, this popular concert venue showcases the newest talents and finest jazz musicians in the country. In addition, it has high-quality acoustics and cozy interior, making it a great place to hang out with friends, old and new alike. Aside from jazz musicians, the venue's stage has also been graced by well-known international and local bands performing a variety of genres, including Bossa Nova, classical music, and salsa.

A melting pot of modern Hungarian artists

What: Fogashaz

Where: Akacfa utca 51, Budapest 1073, Hungary

District VII

Website: http://www.fogashaz.hu/

Phone: +36 70 324 5281

When: 10 am to 4 am from Monday to Saturday. 4 pm to 4 am on Sundays

Why: Fogashaz is an ecstatic fusion of a ruin pub and cultural center, welcoming musicians, theatre groups, and contemporary artists. A variety of late night programs is available throughout the week, such as theater performances and film screenings. A great venue to mingle with the friendly locals, the place has a large atmospheric courtyard with bouncy music from local DJs.

9 BEST DAY TRIPS FROM BUDAPEST

Have an extra day up your sleeve? Then set out and explore the wonders surrounding this great city.

What to see: Memento Park

Why: The park is brimming with mementos of the Soviet-era in the shape of larger-than-life statues, including an amazing 80-foot tall Stalin!

Where: 6 miles south-east of the city

How to get there: Take bus #150 from *Ujbuda Kozpont*, the ride takes about half an hour. Alternatively, you can take the Metro (lines 1, 2 and 3) from Deak Square in Downtown.

Cost: Day bus pass costs 450 HUF, entry to the park 1,500 HUF, and you can take a guided tour in English for an extra 1,200 HUF

Best time to visit: The Park is open from 10 am until sunset and never gets insanely busy, so go at any time

http://www.mementopark.hu/

Fancy going to another country?

It may seem bizarre to recommend you go to a different country once you've made it to Budapest. Yet **Vienna**, the outstanding Austrian capital, is merely a couple of hours away from Budapest so…what better time to visit? It may make for a very long day trip (better stay overnight if you can fit it in) but it's definitely doable and insanely enjoyable.

What to see: Vienna, Austria

Why: For the amazing architecture, stunning historic center and delectable chocolate cake (*sachertorte*)!

How to get there: If heading for a day trip, we recommend you get there by train, which is the fastest mode of transport. Take the Raijet high-speed train and you could be in the Austrian capital in just three hours. Book your return ticket well in advance, from Eurail.

http://tinyurl.com/eurailbudapest

**Please do note that you must be on-board at least 35 minutes before leaving, on an international service.

Cost: Train tickets cost USD 72 for 1st class with seat allocation

Best Time to Visit: To make the most of your day we recommend you board the train at 7am

http://www.vienna.info/en

If you are as besotted as most tourists about the sheer number and quality of Budapest's thermal baths, then you really ought to make a side trip to **Miskolc**, home of the most stunning thermal spa in this whole region.

What to see: Cave Baths of Miskolc

Why: These therapeutic baths are carved out of the mountainside, compliments of Mother Nature. There are several indoor & outdoor pools and a great garden area for sun baking. Top excuse to get out of the hustle of the city!

Where: Miskolc is a one-hour train ride north-east of Budapest and, aside the caves, boasts a wonderful castle and lovely town center.

How to get there: The baths are just 7 kms from Miskolc's town center, which you can reach by InterCity train from Budapest's Keleti Station (2 hours). Once in Miskolc, skip the bus and take a taxi to the baths, as it's cheap, fast and infinitely more convenient.

Cost: Train tickets cost 3, 700 HUF (if bought in advance). Bath entrance fee is 3,500 HUF adult / 2,600 HUG children (no time limit)

Medical treatments – b/w 350 HUF and 1,200 HUF

Wellness treatments b/w 1,000 HUF and 12,000 HUF

Best Time to Visit: NOT on weekends, public holidays, or any day in August!

http://www.barlangfurdo.hu/en/cave-bath

10 A DAY OUT SHOPPING IN BUDAPEST

Budapest has something to offer every shopper, whether it be a designer gear addict, antique lover or used book enthusiast.

Here are the most popular shopping destinations in town:

Vaci Utca Street

The main shopping drag in Budapest, home to designer boutiques and fantastic leather goods stores. Historically, this is one of the oldest trading streets in Hungary and business has been at its very core since the 1700s.

Where: District V

Fashion Street

On the opposite end you have Fashion Street, the 'newest' shopping street, which was created in 2007. This is a 150 m pedestrian extension to Vaci utca and, as the name suggests, offers clothing of all shapes, sizes, and prices.

Where: District V

Grand Boulevard

Nagykörút is, at over 4kms, the longest road in the Hungarian capital and runs through no less than five districts. On the section where the street boasts luxury hotels, namely the Corinthia Royal and New York Palace, the road boasts some rather impressive, albeit expensive, souvenir stores.

Where: District VII

WestEnd City Center

One of the largest shopping malls in all of Central Europe, this place is a mecca for shoppers and fashion lovers. Here you'll find everything you need, with more than 50 jewelry stores, 60 shoe stores, 180 shops, and 300 clothing brands at your beck and call. Best part? It's not the most expensive mall in town!

Where: Ingatlanhasznosito es Uzemelteto Kft., District VI

Contact number: +36 1 374 6573

Opening hours: 8 am to 11 pm daily

Most Authentic Budapest Souvenirs

So what exactly does one bring home from Budapest?

Hungary is renowned for its craftiness so bringing something home to complement your home furnishings is a brilliant idea. Colorful, hand-made and stunning **Herend porcelain** comes in all sorts of lovely treats, like dinner sets, cups, figurines and ornaments; as does **Ajka crystal**, arguably one of Hungary's most prized products. You'll also no doubt come across many **embroidered and laced gems** and **wood-carved artifacts**.

http://www.westend.hu/

11 BUDAPEST LOCAL CUISINE

Hungary was a great empire that spanned many regions of the world, and as a result their foods have a unique variety and flavor shaped from over a thousand years of multicultural tradition. Here are some of the key regional dishes that you can enjoy during your travels to Budapest:

Paprika – Let's start with the basics, shall we? Hungarians are renowned for having a rather healthy obsession with paprika. You'll see peppers stuffed, grilled, roasted, added in every sauce imaginable and, when all is served, ground to a powder and sprinkled on top of a dish. Whichever way you wish to flavor it, make sure to look out for it on restaurant menus.

Goulash – Also popular in Slovakia, Poland, and the Czech Republic, the world-famous goulash has many varieties and, in Hungary, it's considered the national dish. The local version is a stew cooked with dumplings, seasoned beef, and tomatoes, along with plenty of spices, paprika (but of course!) and onions. It's a heavy and very filling meal, so don't eat it before a big hike!

Jokai Bean Soup – A wonderfully aromatic soup made with pork, beans, carrots, and seasoned with lots of parsley and vinegar. Tangy and delicious!

Langos – Commonly regarded as a 'heart attack on a plate', this delicious street treat consists of a deep fried pita or flatbread, which is most frequently eaten with garlic or cheese. It's a greasy but inexpensive and tasty snack.

Kürtőskalács- the Hungarian tube doughnut

Arguably one of the most exported treats to come out of Hungary is this tongue twister of a doughnut, which is baked into a doughy tube and rolled over a mix of sugar and cinnamon. Totally divine, totally addictive and found in every street corner of Buda.

Halászlé (Fisherman's Soup) – As the name suggests, this is not a dish for light-hearted eaters. It's a fish soup seasoned with large amounts of paprika, making it a savory yet spicy dish to enjoy. While it's not quite as extreme as eating a bowl full of peppers, it is a very memorable soup that will delight foodies as well as anyone with a hankering for heat in their cuisine.

Töltött káposzta (Stuffed Cabbage Rolls) – The ingredients used in this dish are simple: rice, cabbage, pork or beef or chicken, traditionally cooked in a tomato based sauce. The combination of these modest ingredients, make for a fantastic healthy and filling meal. The rice is cooked and combined with the pork and then placed into a cabbage leaf and cooked in the tomato base. The flavor is further enhanced by onion, paprika, garlic, and peppers.

Szilvásgombóc (Plum Dumplings) – Take a warm potato dumpling, place juicy plums inside, sprinkle it with cinnamon or sugar and you get this incredible dish, bursting with flavor! If it sounds like a dessert, you'd be surprised to know that it's actually more often served as a main entrée, due to its plentiful calories. Eat a few of these, and lunch is done!

Lecsó – Hungarians like their stews, and this dish is yet another in a long line of many. Lecsó is a thick, simmering mixture of tomatoes, peppers, onions, and paprika. Some varieties add sausage to the mix, giving the stew even more flavor.

Palacsinta (Hungarian Pancake) – So what, do you ask, is the difference between the traditional American Pancake and this Hungarian version? The Hungarian version is a thinner pancake, filled with either cottage cheese or jam, and is rolled into something resembling a pipe. One can then sprinkle sugar or cocoa powder on top for a delicious treat.

Fatányéros (Hungarian Barbecue) – Like most Slavs, the Hungarians like their meat, and this particular dish contains much of it, including grilled pork, beef, veal, as well as bacon and it's served with potatoes and a salad.

12 DINING OUT IN BUDAPEST

Finding a filling and yummy meal in this cosmopolitan destination won't be a problem for any foodie. From Michelin-star restaurants to small cafes and eateries, the city is oozing with dining establishments that serve delectable Hungarian and international dishes.

Insider's Tip: If you happen to be travelling on a tight budget AND are a little adventurous, then look out for daily set-lunch menus offered by many restaurants. Usually, they cost between 1,000 and 2,000 HUF and include a soup, main and small dessert. This is not only a great way to save some forint but also a priceless chance to try dishes you've never savored before.

Cheap & cheerful eats

What: Kisharang Restaurant

Why: Awarded with a certificate of excellence in 2014 by Tripadvisor, Kisharang Restaurant is a small, cozy and unpretentious place with affordable prices, exemplary service and appetizing Hungarian goodies. The Hortobagy pancakes and home-made goulash are particularly well-rated.

Where: 1051 Oktober 6. U. 17, District V

Phone: +36 1 269 3861

How much: Mains hover between 600 and 2,400 HUF

http://www.kisharang.hu/

What: W35

Why: Located right at the heart of Budapest, W35 Restaurant is a classic American street food joint that serves the juiciest and best-tasting burgers and Tex-Mex food in town. Taste buds getting homesick? Get here pronto!

Where: Wessenlenyi utca 35, District VII

Phone: +36 1 796 5370

How much: Mains from 1,400 to 2,200 HUF

https://www.facebook.com/w35streetfood

What: Mamo Gelato Restaurant

Why: Craving for something sweet? Indulge in a nectarous scoop of genuine Italian gelato with a visit to the Mamo Gelato Restaurant. For a small place, the restaurant amazingly has a dozen gelato varieties.

Where: Raday utca 24, District IX

Phone: +36 70 420 4259

How Much: Enjoy a mouthwatering sweet lunch for about 1,400 HUF

http://www.mamogelato.com/

Insider's tip: If you're looking for a cheap eat and a cultural experience bar none, make a point of visiting the Budapest's Grand Central Market Hall. This phenomenal fresh produce market may be a bit out of the way but it's definitely worth seeing (and feasting)! This is the country's oldest and largest indoor marketplace and business has been coming here since the late 1800s. Admiring the stunning building is well worth the trip of its own accord!

What: Great Central Market Hall (Központi Vásárcsarnok)

Why: You'll find a wide array of fresh and cooked local produce, amazing cured meats, cheeses, pickles…as well as flea-market gear of all sorts.

Where: Vamhaz korut 1-3, District IX

Directions: The market is just one block back from

the Danube riverfront, about 2kms south of Chain Bridge. Enjoy a leisurely half hour walk south or reach the market with Tram #2.

When: Mondays 6 am to 5 pm/Tuesday to Friday 6 am to 8 pm/Saturday 6 am to 3 pm

Best time to visit: Early morning for the freshest produce. Two hours should be sufficient time.

http://budapestmarkethall.com/great-market-hall-budapest

Mid-range options

What: Hungarikum Bisztro Restaurant

Why: With its attentive service and remarkable gastronomic pleasures, it is no wonder the Hungarikum Bisztro Restaurant gets a ton of rave reviews from foodies and culinary experts. Often publicized as the premier Hungarian restaurant in Budapest, Hungarikum Bisztro Restaurant also has a dazzling collection of wines, nice live music, and a romantic ambiance. A must try in this restaurant is the flavorful goulash soup with tender beef. Other delightful dishes offered in this restaurant include chicken-filled crepes with paprika sauce, crispy duck legs, and pork loin with tasty fried potatoes.

Where: Steindl Imre utca 13, District V

Phone: +36 30 661 6244

How Much: Enjoy a three-course set Hungarian menu for 4,200 HUF

http://hungarikumbisztro.hu/

What: Curry House Restaurant

Why: Are you in the mood for something unique, healthy and spicy? Delight your taste buds with a true taste of India at the Curry House, the best Indian restaurant in town, where you can feast on scrumptious lamb curries and a myriad of vegetarian dishes.

Where: Horanszky utca 1, District VIII

Phone: +36 1 264 0297

How much: Entrees from 800 HUF and mains b/w 2,000 and 3,000 HUF

http://curryhouse.hu/

What: Taverna Dionysos Restaurant

Why: The Taverna Dionysos Restaurant is a rare gem in the city's rich culinary scene. One of the very few Greek restaurants in the city, Taverna has a pleasant Mediterranean feel and attentive service. More importantly, it has a diverse selection of sumptuous Greek food.

Where: Belgrad Rakpart 16, Belvaros-Lipotvaros,

District V

Phone: +36 1 318 1222

How Much: Appetizers cost about 1,000 HUF and mains hover about 3,000 HUF

http://www.dionysos.hu/index.php/en/welcome

Plush in taste & price

What: Onyx

Why: Onyx is a Michelin-starred restaurant that has added a new twist to the most beloved traditional dishes in the country. Modernizing the country's cuisine, this upscale restaurant delights its guests with its highly acclaimed "Hungarian Evolution", a piquant six-course menu. Furthermore, the restaurant has a beautiful atmosphere coupled with first-class service.

Where: Vorosmarty Square 7 to 8, District V

Phone: +36 30 508 0622

How much: Superlative tasting menus will set you back 28,000 HUF

http://www.onyxrestaurant.hu/

What: Comme Chez Soi Restaurant

Why: As far as Italian cuisine is concerned, Comme Chez Soi Restaurant is absolutely your best bet during your trip to this cosmopolitan hub. Not only does it have an authentic character and nostalgic ambiance, but it also has fast, attentive and efficient service. As for the food, the restaurant will delight you with large servings of your favorite Italian staples and quite a few unique offerings, like a delectable entrée of goose-liver fried with apples. Complementary Hungarian schnapps and homemade lemon sorbet seal the deal.

Where: Aranykez u2, District V

Phone: +36 1 318 3943

How much: Main courses are about 6,000 HUF

http://www.commechezsoi.com/

What: Paris Budapest Bar and Restaurant

Why: A harmonious fusion of Hungarian and French cuisines, the Paris Budapest Bar /and Restaurant is an exclusive joint with amazing views, mouthwatering specialties and fabulous cocktails. Appetizing seafood, including shark, sea razor, octopus, crabs, shrimps and oysters are guaranteed to satisfy discerning foodies, especially in a landlocked country!

Where: Szechenyi Istvan ter 2, Sofitel Budapest Chain Bridge

Phone: +36 30 302 7885

How Much: With starters at 40,000 HUF this meal will not be cheap, but it will be unforgettable.

http://www.parisbudapest.hu/en/restaurant/

Insider's Tip: Happy with the service? Then hand over a few forints to your waiter in hand – do not leave it on the table, as this is considered rue in the local culture!

13 ACCOMMODATION GUIDE

Are you on the lookout for a great place to stay in Budapest? Whether you are self-indulgent or a budget-conscious backpacker, Hungary's capital certainly has an accommodation that fits like a glove to your budget and taste. From the five-star properties and epicurean guesthouses of Buda Hills to the converted flats and hostels of its downtown area, the city of Budapest offers a wide range of accommodations to its trippers.

Budget-friendly accommodations

What: Corvin Point Hostel

Why: The Corvin offers private rooms and apartments as well as 4, 6 and 8-bed dorms and, for the prices, it just can't be beat. Close to transport options, with a great little breakfast cafe next door and offering clean an inexpensive accommodation; this is a wonderful choice for anyone on a tight budget.

Where: Budapest, Nap u. 4, District VIII

Phone: +36 70 544 0224

How much: Prices start from 5,300 HUF

http://www.corvinpoint.com/

What: The Loft Hostel Budapest

Why: Centrally located (just around the corner from the delish Comme Chez Soi Restaurant!), clean, spacious and super friendly, this hostel is perfect for young, carefree backpackers...and the young at heart! Quirky spot and a great home away from home.

Where: Veres Palne Utca 19, 4th floor /6. bell 44, District V

Phone: +36 1328 0916

How much: Dorm prices start from as low as 4,800 HUF

http://www.lofthostel.hu/

What: Agape Guesthouse

Why: Located in the center of town, the Agape Guesthouse is a great base for sightseers who want to be mesmerized by the beautiful heritage sites of the city. The guesthouse offers private rooms with clean bathrooms and a ton of amenities. A few of the rooms boast balconies with striking city views.

Where: Budapest, Akacfa utca 12, District VII

Phone: +36 1 317 4833

How much: At 11,000 HUF, this is a more expensive choice than the others, yet for this you do get a studio for 2 people, as opposed to a dorm bed

http://agapeguesthouse.eu/

Mid-range options

What: Three Corners Hotel Art

Why: Set in the serene side street of Budapest's downtown area, the Three Corners Hotel Art is a stylish budget hotel with an excellent location. As a guest in this hotel, you get easy access to the Danube embankment as well as a handful of restaurants, bars and attractions. Housed in a historic building, this hotel is also fully air-conditioned, and has a number of niceties, including a sauna, fitness room, café, bar and restaurant.

Where: Kirali Pal Utca 12, District V

Phone: +36 1 266 2166

How much: 20,800 HUF for a double room

http://www.threecorners.com

What: Casati Budapest Hotel

Why: The Casati is within walking distance to everything worth visiting and seeing in this city. Besides its ideal location, it is clean and has a very tasteful décor. To add more pleasure to your stay in this hotel, Casati Budapest Hotel also has a relaxing cellar with a massage, fitness and sauna room.

Where: Paulay Ede u. 31, District V

Phone: +36 1 343 1198

How much: Prices from 35,000 HUF for a double room

http://www.casatibudapesthotel.com/

What: Bo18 Hotel Superior

Why: One of top-rated, mid-range hotels in the city, Bo18 Hotel Superior has everything you need for a relaxing stay in Budapest. Known for its high standards in courtesy, cleanliness and comfort, Bo18 Hotel Superior is indeed a quality hotel with spacious rooms, helpful staff, amazing amenities, and a contemporary design.

Where: Vajdahunyad utca 18, District VIII

Phone: +36 1 469 3526

How much: 27,000 HUF for a double room

http://www.bo18hotelbudapest.com/

Deluxe accommodations

What: Hotel Palazzo Zichy

Why: Hotel Palazzo Zichy is, without a doubt, the most romantic and surreal luxury hotel in the city. Famed for its nostalgic charm, the hotel offers a cluster of well-equipped, clean and comfortable rooms with a slew of facilities and amenities.

Where: Budapest, Lorinc pap ter 2, District VIII

Phone: +36 1 235 4000

How much: Double room rates start at 42,000 HUF

http://www.hotel-palazzo-zichy.hu/

What: Four Seasons Hotel Gresham Palace

Why: Touted as the ultimate luxury hotel in Budapest, the Four Seasons Hotel Gresham Palace delights its guests with its refined service, elegant ambiance and central location. Superb in service and amenities, this hotel is hard to fault.

Where: Szechenyi Istvan ter 5-6, District V

Phone: +36 1 268 6000

How much: Room rate start from 103,000 HUF

http://www.fourseasons.com/budapest/

Please do note that, as can be expected, prices vary depending on season and availability so do check ahead before making any firm plans.

14 BUDAPEST TRAVEL ESSENTIALS

Here are key travel essentials to aid you throughout your trip to Budapest:

Money & Currencies

The currency of Hungary is the Hungarian Forint (HUF). You can exchange your EUR or major currencies at money changers or banks into the HUF when you arrive in the country. Many stores in Budapest accept credit cards (Visa and MasterCard, primarily), however inquire within or check the card symbols displayed in the window to confirm your card can be used prior to purchase.

ATMs are widely available, but if you're asking where one is, use the term, "bankomat" or if you want to get more technical, use "bankjegy-automata".

Before using your debit or credit card, make sure that you notify your bank in advance to avoid having your card locked (as a result of fraud protection). You will find that is more economical to use a credit card that has no foreign transaction fees, or your second option would be to withdraw money from an ATM instead of bringing excess cash into the country and exchanging it (although arriving with some cash for emergencies is always a good idea).

Getting Connected

Hungary's country code is 36, so if your family wants to call your hotel in Hungary and they live within the US, they will have to dial: 011 + 36 (country code) + 1 (Budapest's area code) + phone number.

Example:

011 36 1 1234567

Making a call to Budapest from outside of the US/Canada (for example, you are in Europe)? Swap the 011 for 00.

Example:

00 36 1 1234567

If you are in Budapest and need emergency services, the number to dial is 112 for any emergency, 107 if you need the police, 104 if you need an ambulance, and 105 if you need fire services.

If you want to call Hungarian numbers and you are within Hungary, just put in the area code + phone number. Take note of the numbers that start with 0681 and 0690 though, as they represent expensive toll numbers. The toll-free numbers are usually those that start with 0680.

When trying to reach your friends and family back home and calling from a Hungarian phone, just dial the country code + area code + the phone number you need to reach. Note that certain charges may apply if you are calling from your hotel phone.

Tourist Sites

As a visitor, you should note that most of the museums are be closed on Mondays. However, other major sites like the tour of the Parliament, and the Great Synagogue remain open. Monday's are also a good time to visit the parks of Budapest or enjoy one of the many walking tours of the city. Synagogues close early on Friday and are closed on Saturday.

Sights may also be closed depending on religious affiliations – for example, expect some Catholic or Christian sites to be closed on Whitsunday, Good Friday, and Christmas. Additional celebrations to put in your calendar would include the Spring Festival, held in late March, and the Fringe festival, held in early April.

Most shops close early, before 8 pm however they may offer extended hours on Thursdays (until 8 or 9pm). Standard mealtimes are the same as what you may be used to back home: breakfast between 6-10 am, Lunch from 11 am-2 pm, and dinner from 6 pm to 8 pm.

15 HUNGARIAN LANGUAGE ESSENTIALS

Below is a list of key phrases that you might find yourself in need of as a tourist in Budapest. For additional phrases and vocabulary, check out this concise survival dictionary:

http://budapest.travel/info/survivaldic/

Hello.

Szervusz.

(SER-voos)

What is your name?

Hogy hívják?

(hodj HEEV-yak?)

My name is _____ .

_____ vagyok.

(_____ VÅ-djok.)

Please.

Kérem.

(KEY-rem)

Thank you.

Köszönöm.

(KØ-sø-nøm)

* The symbol ø is pronounced like "u" in the English word "f**u**n".

You're welcome.

Szívesen.

(SEE-ve-shen)

Yes.

Igen.

(EE-gen)

No.

Nem.

(nem)

Excuse me. (pardon me)

Bocsánatot kérek.

(BO-cha-nå-tot KEY-rek)

* The symbol å is pronounce like 'o' in the English word "pot"

I'm sorry.

Bocsánat.

(BO-cha-nåt)

Goodbye

Viszontlátásra.

(VEE-sont-la-tash-rå)

Do you speak English?

Beszél angolul?

(BE-seyl ÅN-go-loul?)

Help!

Segítség!

(SHE-geet-sheyg!)

I don't understand.

Nem értem.

(nem EYR-tem)

Where is the toilet?

Hol van a mosdó?

(hol vån å MOSH-doa?)

It's an emergency.

Vészhelyzet van.

(VEYS-hey-zet vån)

I'm lost.

Eltévedtem.

(EL-tey-ved-tem)

I lost my bag.

Elveszett a táskám.

(EL-ve-set å TASH-kam)

Numbers

1 egy (edj)

2 kettő (kApter)

3 három (HA-rom)

4 négy (neydj)

5 öt (øt)

6 hat (håt)

7 hét (heyt)

8 nyolc (nyolts)

9 kilenc (KEE-lents)

10 tíz (teez)

Shopping

How much is this?

Mennyibe kerül?

(MEN-nyi-be KE-růl)

That's too expensive.

Az túl drága.

(åz tool DRA-gå)

expensive

drága

(DRA-gå)

cheap

olcsó

(OL-choa)

Important Signs & Their Meanings

NYITVA Open

ZÁRVA Closed

BEJÁRAT Entrance

KIJÁRAT Exit

TOLNI Push

HÚZNI Pull

MOSDÓ Toilet

FÉRFI Men

NŐ Women

TILOS Forbidden

CONCLUSION

Budapest is a Hungarian dream full of life and off the beaten path surprises. Known as one of the most delightful cities in Europe, this beautiful grand-dame has the grandeur and grace of the continent's two most glamorized destinations, Vienna and Paris, whilst still very much infusing an eastern flavor at every turn.

From sightseeing to shopping, there are a lot of things you can do and enjoy in Budapest in 72 hours or less. Whether you are fond of art, culture, partying, history or contemporary engineering masterpieces, a three-day trip to this city gives you a plethora of joyous memories that you'll cherish for years to come. But, if you want to extend your stay, and discover more of the city, go ahead, and enjoy the rest Budapest has to offer.

Bucsu!

15088334R00059

Printed in Great Britain
by Amazon.co.uk, Ltd.,
Marston Gate.